Castletown, Co. Kildare

Patrick Walsh

Introduction

This I believe the only house in Ireland to which the term palace can be applied.

Richard Twiss, 1775

Built between 1722 and 1729 for William Conolly, Speaker of the Irish House of Commons and the wealthiest commoner in Ireland, Castletown is Ireland's largest and earliest Palladian style house. The facade was almost certainly designed by the Italian architect Alessandro Galilei, while the Irish architect Sir Edward Lovett Pearce added the wings. The house remained in the hands of the Speaker's descendants until 1965 when it was purchased by a property developer, Major Willson. Fortunately, the house was saved in 1967 when, along with 120 acres of the demesne lands, it was purchased for £93,000 by Desmond Guinness, co-founder of the Irish Georgian Society. The house was opened to the public in the same year and restoration work began, funded by the Irish Georgian Society and private benefactors. In 1979, care of the house passed to the Castletown Foundation, a charitable trust established to own, maintain and continue the restoration of the house. In the early 1990s the Castletown Foundation realised that the roof, stone cornice and balustrade of the main block required urgent and extensive repairs. Following discussions with Government, the house (with the exception of its contents), its immediate setting, the Celbridge Avenue and the Connolly Folly were transferred to state care in 1994. Work began immediately on the repair of the external fabric of the building, structural repairs and upgrading of building services. Castletown is now managed by the Office of Public Works. Through restoration, conservation, acquisition of parkland and development of visitor facilities, the long-term objective is to preserve for future generations one of the most important houses in Ireland and one of significance in terms of European architectural heritage.

GROUND FLOOR WITH
KITCHEN WING (LEFT)
STABLE WING (RIGHT)

FIRST FLOOR PLAN

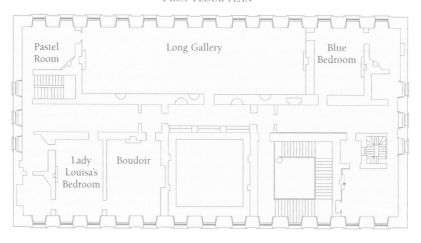

Pastel Room

Long Gallery

Blue Bedroom

Lady Louisa's Bedroom

Boudoir

GROUND FLOOR PLAN

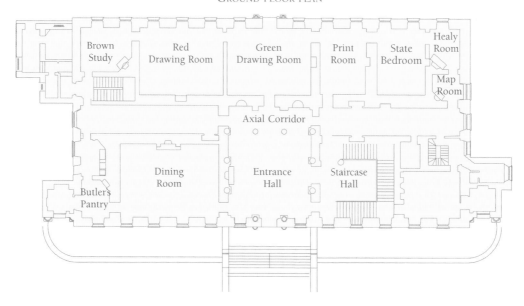

Brown Study

Red Drawing Room

Green Drawing Room

Print Room

State Bedroom

Healy Room

Map Room

Axial Corridor

Butler's Pantry

Dining Room

Entrance Hall

Staircase Hall

Architectural History

'The most remarkable thing now going on is a house of Mr Conolly's at Castletown, it is 142 feet in front and above 60 in the clear, the height will be about 70. It is to be of fine wrought stone, harder and better coloured than the Portland, with outhouses joining to it by colonnades, etc. The plan is chiefly of Mr Conolly's invention, however, in some points they have been pleased to consult me.'
Bishop Berkeley 1722

Castletown, as Ireland's first and largest Palladian style house, is an important part of our country's architectural heritage. Erected between 1722 and 1729, Castletown was built with two wings connected by Ionic colonnades flanking the Italian Renaissance-inspired central block of the house. The wings, in true Palladian fashion, contained the kitchens on one side and the stables on the other. This style had originated in Italy with the 16th-century architect Andrea Palladio (1508-80), and had come to prominence in England in the early 18th century. The original interior layout of the house owed much to recently published plans of English houses such as Chevening in Kent, with a central hall and saloon surrounded by four apartments on the ground floor and a gallery flanked by apartments on the *piano nobile* level. This primacy of the first floor was emphasised by longer widows on the facade. The lengthening of the ground-floor windows later in the century distorted this effect. The layout reflected Conolly's vision of the house as a venue for large-scale political entertaining.

The identity of the architect of the house is still subject to debate, but the facade, built of Edenderry limestone, is by the Italian architect Alessandro Galilei (1691-1737) whom Conolly had met when the former visited Ireland in 1718-19. When construction began three years later, Galilei had returned to Italy, and it is unclear whether his plans were followed. Instead, it seems likely that Conolly sought advice from a number of local connoisseurs including the philosopher, George Berkeley, who had recently returned from an extensive Italian grand tour, and the architect Thomas Burgh. The initial building work may have been overseen by Irish master builder John Rothery, later architect of Mount Ievers, Co. Clare. Mount Ievers shares a number of features with Castletown including the two gigantic chimney stacks, the plain

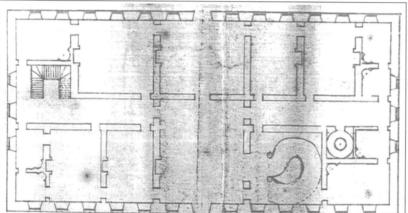

ABOVE LEFT: *Alessandro Galilei*, by Guiseppe Berti.
MIDDLE: *Speaker William Conolly*, c. 1729, by Charles Jervas.
ABOVE RIGHT: *Lady Louisa Conolly*, c. 1770, wife of Thomas Conolly, by Hugh Douglas Hamilton.
LEFT: Ground floor plan of the interior layout of the house by Edward Lovett Pearce. Note Pearce's original plan for a circular staircase (V&A).
BELOW: The earliest known drawing of Castletown, by an English visitor, Thomas Wright, who came to the house in 1746/7 (Avery Architectural and Fine Arts Library, Columbia University).

LEFT: Horse and cart at the front steps c. 1880, and detail
of the balustrade and front steps at Castletown.
BELOW: Map of Castletown demesne, c. 1739.

unembellished facade and the corner fireplaces.
Edward Lovett Pearce, the young Irish architect, added
the service wings and the colonnades upon his return
from his Grand Tour in Italy, where, in 1724-25, he
had met Galilei in Florence. He also seems to have
been responsible for the interior layout of the house,
and a ground floor plan survives among his papers.
Pearce (1699-1733), who also designed the Irish House
of Commons in College Green (a commission he
secured partly through Conolly's patronage), was the
leading architect in Ireland in the early 18th century.
His addition of the Ionic colonnades and the Palladian
style wings was to influence the design of many of the
great 18th-century Irish houses such as Carton, Co.
Kildare and Russborough, Co. Wicklow, both designed
by his assistant and successor Richard Castle (c. 1690-
1751).

Castletown underwent a radical architectural
transformation following the arrival of Lady Louisa
Conolly in 1759. Over the next 40 years, she spent
over £25,000 on improvements to the house and
demesne. Guided by her brother-in-law, the 1st Duke
of Leinster, and the published designs of leading British
architects Sir William Chambers (1723-96) and Isaac
Ware, Lady Louisa altered the layout of the interior.
She remodelled the main reception rooms, including
the dining room, the two drawing rooms and the
magnificent long gallery, as well as the great staircase
which was built in 1759. She also altered the front
facade of the house, lengthening most of the ground
floor windows to fit in with contemporary fashion,
thus giving the ground floor equal emphasis. These
changes reflected the changing function of the house as
the Conollys made it their permanent residence. A
constant stream of informal visits replaced the political
congresses intended by Speaker Conolly, and later
hosted by his wife. Following Lady Louisa's death in
1821, few substantive architectural changes were made
to the house. Ambitious plans to cover in the stable

yard behind the east wing were drawn up in the 1850s for Tom Conolly (1823-76), but never carried out. The main reception rooms were, however, extensively redecorated, probably in the 1850s. This work included the conversion of the State Bedroom into a library and the Print Room into a billiard room, as well as the replacement of the silk in the drawing rooms. The Long Gallery was also extensively renovated, and the first floor of the east wing was extensively remodelled in 1871.

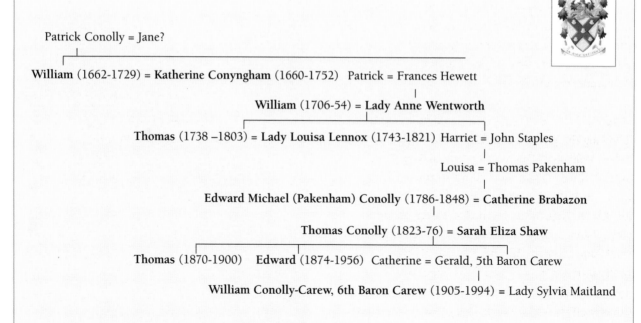

FAMILY TREE

Patrick Conolly = Jane?

William (1662-1729) = Katherine Conyngham (1660-1752) Patrick = Frances Hewett

William (1706-54) = Lady Anne Wentworth

Thomas (1738 –1803) = Lady Louisa Lennox (1743-1821) Harriet = John Staples

Louisa = Thomas Pakenham

Edward Michael (Pakenham) Conolly (1786-1848) = Catherine Brabazon

Thomas Conolly (1823-76) = Sarah Eliza Shaw

Thomas (1870-1900) **Edward (1874-1956)** Catherine = Gerald, 5th Baron Carew

William Conolly-Carew, 6th Baron Carew (1905-1994) = Lady Sylvia Maitland

Castletown owners in bold. Lord Carew sold Castletown in 1965.

The Conolly Family and Castletown; the first 100 years, 1722-1821

William Conolly was born in Ballyshannon, Co Donegal in 1662, the son of a local innkeeper. From such humble origins, he rose to become the wealthiest, most powerful politician in Ireland. The Conollys were presumably of Catholic Irish background although it is likely the family had converted to Protestantism sometime before William's birth. He trained as an attorney in Dublin, where he practiced law in the 1680s. His career, however, only took off following the Williamite war of 1688-91.

In 1689, Catholic James II of England fled to Ireland following the 'glorious revolution' which swept his son-in-law, William of Orange, to power in Britain and Ireland. King William pursued his rival to Ireland, where, in 1690-91, decisive battles were fought at Derry, the Boyne, Aughrim and Limerick. Conolly proceeded to make the most of the opportunities created by the Williamite victory in Ireland. William of Orange confiscated the lands of James' Catholic supporters and it was through dealing in these forfeited estates that Conolly established his fortune. By 1703, he had spent over £10,000 acquiring more than 15,000 acres across seven counties. By any standards, he had generated an immense fortune in a remarkably short period of time.

Conolly's success was, however, partly based on the advantages of a successful marriage. In 1694, he had married Katherine Conyngham, the daughter of a Williamite hero, Sir Albert Conyngham. Like Conolly, she was from Donegal, though of higher social status so his marriage allied Conolly with many of the leading families in Ulster. In addition to her connections and strong personality, she brought a marriage portion of £2,300 which Conolly promptly invested in forfeited land. Not all of his dealings were based on such legitimate grounds. In 1700, he featured in a singular case, involving impersonation and body-snatching, in order to pursue a fraudulent claim for a mortgage worth £12,000, demonstrating the lengths he was prepared to go to secure a favourable deal.

While Conolly increased his private wealth and status, he also began to emerge as an important public figure. In 1692, he was elected to the Irish Parliament for the town of Donegal. He would remain a member of the Irish House of Commons until 1729. In 1715, upon the accession of King George I, he was appointed Speaker of the House of Commons. As Speaker, Conolly acted as chairman of the House of Commons. His role was not to be impartial, but to act as the chief government representative in the Commons. His growing political influence was rewarded in 1717 when he was appointed one of three Lord Justices who would run the country in the absence of the Viceroy. At a time when Sir Robert Walpole was establishing himself as the first Prime Minister in England, Conolly was doing something similar in Ireland.

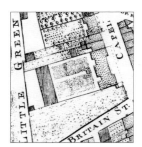

Conolly's own perception of his wealth and status can perhaps be best seen in his building projects. He acquired his first Dublin house in 1707 on Capel Street, which was then the fashionable centre of Dublin. Conolly's house was by far the largest on the street, probably similar in scale to the main block of Castletown. He also continued to amass further properties. In 1718, he purchased an estate of 18,000 acres in Ballyshannon, thus buying his home town. In 1723, he acquired Rathfarnham Castle in Co. Dublin although neither he nor any of his descendants ever lived there. By his death, he owned over 100,000 acres and enjoyed an annual income of almost £17,000 a year making him the wealthiest and the most powerful politician in Ireland. Castletown would become the symbol of his great wealth.

Conolly's death in October 1729 was marked by public pageantry on a grand scale. In his will he left £1,000 to cover the costs of his funeral, as well as various sums for his friends and family to buy mourning rings. His funeral, as described in the *Dublin Weekly Journal* of 8 November 1729, was very elaborate and was attended by all the Members of Parliament, the Lord Lieutenant, Lord Mayor and various nobility and gentry. There were also 67 poor men dressed in black, signifying

Conolly's age. Everybody in the procession wore linen scarves of Irish manufacture, a gesture of support to the Irish linen industry and also the initiation of a custom which would continue into the 20th century.

Conolly's greatest misfortune was perhaps his failure to produce an heir. This lack of an heir meant that upon his death his estates and fortune were divided between his widow Katherine and his nephew William James Conolly, the son of his younger brother, Patrick. In 1734, William Conolly Junior married Lady Anne Wentworth, the daughter of the Earl of Strafford. They lived in Leixlip Castle until the death of Katherine in 1752, thus beginning the long and continuing association between Castletown and Leixlip Castle.

Sadly, Speaker Conolly spent little time at Castletown, as public duties usually detained him in Dublin, although in the last year of his life he spent more time there as his health worsened. Even in its unfinished state, the house attracted important visitors. The Lord Lieutenant spent Christmas at Castletown, while in 1725 a Dublin Castle official fell to his death when viewing the still incomplete house from scaffolding. It was only after the Speaker's death that the house began to be fully used in the manner he had intended. His wife continued to act as a political hostess, throwing lavish parties at Castletown to perpetuate her husband's memory. Castletown became a fashionable place to be seen and was regarded as a rival to the

LEFT: Detail from a portrait of William Conolly Junior, by Anthony Lee (NGI).
MIDDLE: Thomas Conolly, Speaker Conolly's grand-nephew who inherited Castletown in 1754, by Hugh Douglas Hamilton.

BELOW: Lord Edward FitzGerald, leader of the 1798 rebellion and nephew of Lady Louisa Conolly, by Hugh Douglas Hamilton.

Vice-Regal Court in Dublin Castle. In the early 1730s, Katherine effectively ran a casino in the house when Lord Lieutenant Dorset banned gambling. Carriage races along the avenue were also a feature of Castletown entertainments, and Katherine partook fully in these activities with a host of rakish young men. Upon her death in 1752, at the age of 90, it was lamented that the huge house, that used to be crowded with guests of all sorts, was empty and forlorn. Mrs Delany's tribute gives some indication of Katherine Conolly's virtues as a hostess: *We have lost our great Mrs Conolly. She died last Friday and is a general loss. Her table was open to all friends of all ranks and her purse to the poor. She was I think in her ninetieth year. She had been dropping for some years, but never too ill to shut out company.*

Katherine Conolly's longevity meant that the Speaker's nephew, also named William, only inherited Castletown in 1752. Unfortunately, he died two years later and was succeeded by his son Thomas who was still a minor. Thomas Conolly (1738-1803) arrived at Castletown in 1759 following his marriage to Lady Louisa Lennox (1743-1821) in 1758. Lady Louisa, the third of the famous daughters of the Duke of Richmond, had spent much of her childhood at Carton near Maynooth, the home of her sister Emily, Duchess of Leinster. Her elder sister, Caroline, married the leading English politician Henry Fox, while her younger sister, Sarah, led a turbulent private life before eventually settling down in 1781 at Oakley Park in Celbridge. Lady Louisa had no children and instead devoted much of her energies to improvements to the house and demesne at Castletown. The Staircase Hall, Dining Room, Print Room and Long Gallery are among the rooms that can be considered symbols of her contribution to the house. In these years, Castletown again became a lively, hospitable place, with a constant stream of visitors which included the Lord Lieutenant and London actress, Sarah Siddons. Through both her correspondence with her sisters and the meticulously kept household accounts, a vast amount of information has survived about Castletown in the mid- to late 18th century.

Thomas Conolly was the quintessential Irish gentleman, a keen huntsman and a fine horseman, as well as a politician and landowner. Regarded as the wealthiest commoner in the kingdom, he actually spent much of his career in debt because of large debts he inherited from his father. Conolly sat in the Irish parliament for 40 years where he prided himself on his often imagined independence. His character and temperament, however, did not always lend themselves to political success. He usually tended towards indecision and rarely grasped opportunities that came his way. Although a patriot in the broadest sense of the word, Conolly was a strong supporter of the Act of Union in 1800. This support for the Union, which extinguished the independent Irish parliament in College Green, was partly influenced by the 1798 rebellion which had a profound effect on the extended Conolly/ FitzGerald family. At Castletown, 12 servants and footmen were dismissed for involvement in the rebellion. The

Conollys were deeply shocked by the attitude of their tenants, considering the good relations they had always enjoyed with them. Worse was to come, however, with the tragic death of Lady Louisa's favourite nephew, the United Irishman leader, Lord Edward FitzGerald. She was among the last people to see him before his death in Newgate Gaol in May 1798. At the other end of the political spectrum was Thomas Conolly's nephew, Lord Castlereagh, the Chief Secretary, who was entrusted with quashing the rebellion and introducing the Act of Union.

Thomas Conolly's political career ended with the Union, and, disillusioned with life in Ireland, the family contemplated leaving Castletown. Following his death in 1803, Lady Louisa considered selling the house for use as a barracks to alleviate some debts, but the Barrack Board was not interested and turned down the offer. Lady Louisa changed her lifestyle and devoted the remaining years of her life to charitable works instead of improvements to the house and estate. Among her achievements was the establishment of a school on the site of her husband's kennels inside the gates of Castletown. A new Protestant church was also erected inside the gates to replace the earlier church which had been destroyed in the 1798 rebellion. She survived her husband by 18 years, dying in August 1821. Her nephew, George Napier, left the following account of her funeral which captures the esteem in which Lady Louisa was held by her tenantry and servants:

> …as soon as day light appeared, the people began to collect in the park in front of the house …many thousands were assembled…many from thirty and forty miles off, so well was she known…I ordered the great door to be thrown open and the procession moved from the hall…the moment the body appeared…one long loud cry of despair issued from the assembled multitude…the coffin was lowered into the vault; then again that thrilling cry was heard, but louder and longer…a general rush was made to the vault, each striving to get a last look at the coffin which contained the remains of One they almost revered as a saint.

Castletown and the Conollys in the 19th century and beyond, 1821-1965

Lady Louisa's death in 1821 ended an era at Castletown. The Conolly estates, including Castletown, were inherited by Thomas Conolly's grand-nephew Edward Pakenham (1786-1848). Under the terms of Conolly's will, Edward was required to change his name to Conolly. Thomas Conolly had also hoped and recommended that his heirs 'will be resident in Ireland as their ancestor, Mr Speaker Conolly, the original and honest maker of my fortune, was'. The estates Edward Conolly inherited were heavily encumbered, and the family's fortunes declined financially as well as politically. Changes to the house in this period seem to have been minimal. In the 18th century, Castletown was the main residence of the Conolly family, but after the Act of Union in 1800, Dublin declined as a political and social centre. From 1830, Edward Conolly spent much of his time in London attending parliament, and Castletown was used as a country retreat. At Westminster, he often spoke on Irish affairs telling the House of Commons in 1847 during the great famine to 'throw political economy to the wind and listen to the starving people'. Returning to Castletown, he contributed to the local relief effort and donated land for the Celbridge workhouse. Few changes were made to the house in this period, other than the provision of a nursery and a schoolroom for his ten children, probably due to the straightened economic circumstances.

In 1848, Edward Conolly was succeeded at Castletown and Westminster by his eldest son, Thomas. The five younger sons pursued other careers. The fourth brother, Colonel John Augustus Conolly of the Coldstream Guards, was one the first winners of the Victoria Cross in the Crimean war. 'Tom' Conolly's succession heralded a new era at Castletown. As a young man he had spent much time in London and on

BELOW LEFT: Sarah Eliza Shaw, the Celbridge miller's daughter who married Tom Conolly in 1869, by William Osborne. (Courtesy of Christies Images).

BELOW RIGHT: Photograph of Tom and Sarah Eliza Conolly c. 1875.

the continent living the high life. Among his acquaintances on the continent was the future French Emperor, Napoleon III. In 1864, Conolly, continuing his thirst for adventure, travelled to Virginia at the height of the American Civil War where he met General Lee, Jefferson Davis and other Confederate leaders. Upon his return to Ireland he settled down at Castletown in 1869, marrying Sarah Eliza Shaw, the Celbridge miller's daughter. Castletown, once again, became known for its hospitality. Improvements were made to the house, including the decoration of the Blue Bedroom, the partial redecoration of the Long Gallery and the Red and Green Drawing Rooms. Conolly's sporting interests could be seen in the conversion of the Print Room into a billiards room and the creation of a smoking room for hunting parties

above the stables. Some indication of life at Castletown during this time can be gained from the following description, by Elizabeth Smith, of a party held in February 1853:

Tom Conolly did it admirably well – engaged a special train to carry his company to Hazelhatch and back, had omnibuses there to bring them on, the one for the ladies, new lined with glazed cotton to save their dresses. About two hundred people, Hanlon's Band, the whole house thrown open, quantities of refreshments and a good supper. It was all very charming! But considering they had to be dressed by nine, were to be an hour on the way, that it was a perfect storm of snow, and they returned home at seven in the morning, I can't help but think that us who were all the while snug in bed were in a better place.

'Tom' Conolly, the last of the family to serve in parliament, died in 1876 aged only 53. He was succeeded by his eldest son also named Thomas, who was only six when his father died. A captain in the British Army, he was killed in the Boer War in 1900, and was succeeded by his brother, Major Edward Conolly. Major Conolly did not settle down at Castletown until after the First World War. In the intervening period Castletown was let to a series of tenants, especially for the hunting season, including Lord Peter 'Packer'

TOP LEFT: The Dining Room c. 1900 (IAA).
BOTTOM LEFT: The Long Gallery c. 1900 (IAA).
RIGHT: The Staircase Hall c. 1900. Note the two paintings inserted into the plasterwork, one of which is now missing. (IAA).

17

RIGHT: The Dining Room and a view of the Entrance Hall from the staircase, c. 1880.
BELOW: The Castletown hunt, c. 1768, by Robert Healy.

O'Brien, the Wills family, and an American businessman, Tom Kelly, who entertained on a grand scale around the turn of the century. Castletown in these years briefly returned to its 'ancient grandeur.'

Castletown survived through the years of the War of Independence and the Civil War, when other Kildare houses were being burnt down. Indeed, Castletown had a lucky escape in 1922 when republicans, about to set 50 gallons of petrol alight, were dissuaded by a local republican leader who told them: 'on no account was the house to be touched, that it had been built with Irish money by William Conolly who was Speaker of the Irish House of Commons two hundred years or so ago'. In the years following Independence, the Castletown estate continued to provide a major source of local employment particularly in the market

gardens, although the number of in-house servants declined especially after the closure of the great kitchens in the 1930s. Major Conolly, a bachelor, died in 1956 and the house was inherited by his nephew Lord Carew, who took the name Conolly-Carew. The esteem the local workmen held for their landlord was demonstrated at Major Conolly's funeral when the Catholic workmen carried his body into the Protestant church despite the local priest's objections. As one of them later pointed out, 'sure wasn't he the only one who was willing to give us a day's work'. The Conolly-Carews were unable to afford the upkeep of the house, which needed extensive repair work, and put it up for sale in 1965. The house and estate at Castletown were purchased by developer, Major Willson, in 1965, while the contents were auctioned in March 1966.

The Restoration of Castletown

Following the sale of the house and the dispersal of the contents, the house was left vacant and subjected to vandalism: lead was stripped from the roof, and windows were broken. Miraculously, the remaining fittings, including all the original chimney pieces, remained. An inglorious end to Castletown's proud history seemed inevitable. However, in 1967, Desmond Guinness purchased the house and 120 acres of land to save it for posterity. Castletown became the flagship project of the Irish Georgian Society, which had been re-established by Desmond and Mariga Guinness in 1958. In 1967, it became the first house in Leinster to be opened to the public.

The restoration of Castletown began under the aegis of the Irish Georgian Society. Their first major task was to acquire furniture and paintings for the house. Many of the original furnishings had been secured for the house before the auction by Desmond Guinness. Gradually, the Irish Georgian Society, and after 1979 the Castletown Foundation, began to acquire Irish furniture and paintings for the house, through gifts and loans. The restoration of the interior of the house to its 18th-century grandeur began in 1985, with the re-decoration of the Green Drawing Room, which was a notable achievement. The house remained open while the restoration process continued, still mainly funded by private munificence and visitor revenue.

In 1994, the house was taken over by the Irish government and it is now under the management of the Office of Public Works. The Castletown Foundation continues to have an advisory role with regard to the interior and still owns most of the original contents. Since 1994, the conservation process has continued at a faster pace. Major structural work was carried out, particularly on the roof, but also inside the house, in the mid-1990s. Since then, further conservation work has been ongoing, both on the internal fabric of the house and on the contents.

LEFT: The Entrance Hall, with a view towards the Axial Corridor.
BELOW RIGHT: The Entrance Hall with a view through to the
Staircase Hall from a photograph taken c. 1900 (IAA).

The Entrance Hall

The Entrance Hall, designed by Edward Lovett Pearce, is one of the finest features in the house. Two storeys high, it immediately gives the impression of the grandeur that is evident throughout the house. In the 18th century, the hall would have been the hub of everyday life with servants passing along the Axial Corridor at the rear and visitors waiting to be received in the state rooms. By the early 20th century, the hall had become an informal reception room and was filled with furniture. It has since been put back to its original state.

The polished limestone floor with its chequered design and the polished Kilkenny limestone chimney piece reflect Conolly's desire, at the instigation of Bishop Berkeley, to build the house solely of native Irish materials. The decoration of the hall was influenced by the 16th-century Italian villas designed by Andrea Palladio, which Pearce had studied on his Grand Tour. The Ionic columns on the ground level are very similar to the pillars in the colonnades outside, while on the upper level there are tapering pilasters with baskets of fruit and flowers. These baskets, carved in wood but painted to give the impression of plaster, along with the shell motif on the ceiling, have been seen as

21

symbols of wealth and prosperity. The ceiling, with its strongly cornered coving and central roundel followed the neo-Palladian formula that was established in the 1720s, inspired by Inigo Jones' work. The plain plasterwork is traditionally whitewashed and its domestic simplicity is in sharp contrast to the grandeur of Pearce's columnar screen, which divides the Axial Corridor from the hall.

PAINTINGS

View of Leixlip Castle and the Salmon Leap. Mural by Joseph Tudor (1685-1759).*
Alessandro Galilei, 1735, by Giuseppe Berti.

SCULPTURE

Marble bust of George Washington, c. late 18th century, by the studio of Jean Antoine Houdon (1741-1828). Original to Castletown, it was purchased to show the Conollys' sympathy for the colonists during the American War of Independence.
Pair of marble busts of the Earl and Countess of Dartrey, c. 1839.

FURNITURE

George I Irish walnut side table with green marble top with carved moulded frieze, with foliate hairy hoof feet.
English white marble slab table with carved mask of Vesta.
Set of three Irish mahogany hall chairs. Copies of set originally made for Castletown.
George III leather hall porter's chair.*

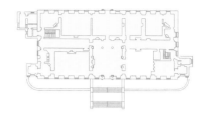

BOTTOM RIGHT: Detail of the Rococo plasterwork by Philip Lafranchini showing a bust of Emily, Duchess of Leinster.

The Staircase Hall

'The staircase is extremely handsome and the geometrical steps, the boldest lightest and best I believe I have seen, the brass balustrade completes the whole giving an elegance quite new to me.'
Charles Cockerell 1825

The Portland stone staircase at Castletown is one of the largest stairs in Ireland. It was built in 1759 under the direction of the master builder Simon Vierpyl (c.1725-1811). Prior to this, the space was a shell, although a plan attributed to Lovett Pearce suggests that a circular staircase was previously intended.

The solid brass balustrade was installed by Anthony King, later Lord Mayor of Dublin. He signed and dated three of the banisters, 'A. King Dublin 1760'. His bill for £280 survives in the household accounts. Work was carried out on the staircase by the Irish Georgian Society in 1977.

The opulent Rococo plasterwork was created by the Swiss-Italian stuccadore Philip Lafranchini, who, with his older brother Paul, had worked at Carton and Leinster House for Lady Lousia's brother-in-law, the 1st Duke of Leinster, as well as at Russborough in Co.

23

Wicklow. Shells, cornucopias, dragons and masks are included in the light-hearted decoration which represents the final development of the Lafranchini style. Family portraits are also included, with Tom Conolly at the foot of the stairs and Lady Louisa above to his right. The four seasons are represented on the piers and on either side of the arched screen.

> **PAINTING**
> *The Bear Hunt*, c. 17th century. Attributed to Flemish artist Paul De Vos (1596-1672).*

The Dining Room

The Dining Room was originally two panelled rooms, forming an apartment, possibly the private quarters of Katherine Conolly. These two rooms were converted by Lady Louisa into a formal dining room in the 1760s. Dining had always played an important part in the hospitality offered at Castletown as the following description, by Mrs Delany, of Katherine's dining habits suggests: *'She generally had two tables of eight or ten people each. Her own table was served with seven courses and a dessert, and two substantial dishes on the sidetable, and if the greatest person in the kingdom dined with her, she never altered her bill-of-fare.'* Lady Louisa continued to entertain in a similar fashion, albeit in a slightly more relaxed fashion: '…*the Gentlemen sat a good while after dinner, and we got our works, and sat around the table and chatted.'*

The Dining Room was completed in 1768 with Lady Louisa taking advice from her brother-in-law James, 1st Duke of Leinster. The ceiling, inspired by Inigo Jones' Banqueting Hall at Whitehall, is based on that in the Leinster House dining room designed by Isaac Ware. Recent colour analysis of the paintwork has revealed that the room was always painted green, while the present shade represents a possible late 18th-century scheme. The plasterwork has also recently been restored. The three giltwood pier glasses with their elaborate frames, featuring symbols of Bacchus and festivity are by the leading Dublin carver, Richard Cranfield (1713-1809).

BELOW LEFT: One of a pair of 19th-century Georgian style mahogany side tables.
BELOW RIGHT: One of a pair of Meissen gilt campana vases, reputedly wedding presents to Tom Conolly (1823-76) from Napoleon III, Emperor of France.

FURNITURE

Pair of George III giltwood serving tables.*
Pair of 19th-century Georgian style mahogany side stables.
20th-century copy of an Irish Georgian mahogany hunt or 'wake' table. Made by James Hicks of Dublin.
The 12 Chippendale mahogany dining chairs are early 20th-century copies of Castletown originals.*
Pair of Meissen gilt campana vases, c. 19th century reputedly wedding presents to Thomas Conolly (1823-76) from Napoleon III, Emperor of France.*

PAINTINGS

Speaker William Conolly (1662-1729). Posthumous portrait by Stephen Catterson Smith (1806-1872).*
Charles, 2nd Duke of Richmond, by Jean-Baptiste Van Loo.*
Father of Louisa Conolly and Emily, Duchess of Leinster. This portrait formerly hung at Carton, Co. Kildare. It was purchased by Lord Carew in 1949 for £4.

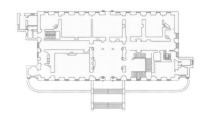

The Butler's Pantry

The Butler's Pantry dates from the 1760s and connected the newly created Dining Room with the kitchens in the west wing. Food would have been carried in from the kitchens through the colonnade passageway and then reheated in the Pantry before being served. The great kitchens were on the ground floor of the wing, with servants' quarters upstairs. Upwards of 80 servants would have been employed in the house and kitchens in the late 18th century under the direction of the butler and the housekeeper, although this number declined by the early 19th century.

The walls of the Pantry are decorated with 19th-century photographs of the Castletown servants and illustrated public addresses to the Conolly family from their tenants. There is also a portrait of a Mrs Parnell Moore, reputedly an 18th-century housekeeper at Castletown.

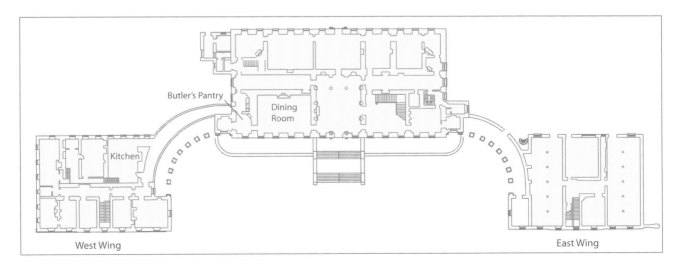

OPPOSITE: A piece of the Volunteer fabric depicting the review of the Leinster Volunteers in the Phoenix Park in 1782.

The Axial Corridor

Pearce's spinal corridor seems to have been influenced by the published designs of Coleshill house in Wiltshire, and is unusual in an Irish context. The Axial Corridor divided the front of the house from the state rooms at the rear. It would have been used by the servants, and many of the doors opening on to the corridor were servants' or jib doors which were not always visible on the other side. This scheme was repeated by Richard Castle at Leinster House in 1745, acknowledged to be the inspiration for the White House. Castletown could claim to be the grandfather of the American presidential residence.

PAINTINGS
Collection of 18th- and 19th-century portraits of the Rossmore family.
Portraits of Paul and Elizabeth Barry by George Mulvany (1809-69).

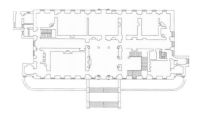

The Brown Study

The Brown Study, with its wood-panelled walls, tall oak doors, corner chimney piece, built-in desk and vaulted ceiling, is decorated as it was in the 1720s when the house was first built. This room was originally used as a bedroom or closet and then later as a breakfast parlour in the early 20th century.

Between the windows is a piece of the Volunteer fabric. Printed on a mixture of linen and cotton, in Harpur's Mills in nearby Leixlip, it depicts the review of the Leinster Volunteers in the Phoenix Park in 1782. Thomas Conolly was active in the Volunteer leadership in both Counties Derry and Kildare. The Volunteers were a local militia force established during the American War of Independence to defend Ireland from possible French invasion, while the regular troops were in America. They were later linked to the 'Patriot' party in the Irish House of Commons led by Henry Grattan, and their campaigns for political reform.

FURNITURE
Oak deed chest inscribed with William Conolly's name.*
A built-in late Georgian mahogany bookcase.*
A Georgian Irish mahogany side table.
A pair of 19th-century oak dining chairs in the Jacobean style.

PAINTINGS
King William of Orange, by Garrett Morphey (d. 1716). Reputedly a present from the sitter to William Conolly.*
Modern Midnight Conversation, after William Hogarth.*
Thomas Wentworth, after Sir Anthony Van Dyck. The sitter was an ancestor of Lady Anne Conolly.*
Dean Jonathan Swift, after Francis Bindon (1690-1765).

The Red Drawing Room

'…withdrawing room covered in a four coloured damask predominantly in red.'
Lady Shelburne 1769.

The Red or Crimson Drawing Room was one of the main reception rooms at the back of the house. Originally laid out as a common parlour with an entrance on to the west corridor, Lady Louisa redecorated it between 1764 and 1768. The neo-classical ceiling, which replaced the coved original, is based on published designs by the Italian Renaissance architect, Sebastiano Serlio. The early 18th-century oak panelling was covered with a four-coloured silk damask. The present red silk dates from the mid-19th century, when the room was extensively refurbished. The Aubusson carpet also dates from this time and was probably made for the room. The white Carrara chimney pieces in the two drawing rooms came to the house in 1768, while the woodwork in both rooms is by Richard Cranfield.

PAINTINGS

Charles James Fox (1749-1806), circle of Sir Joshua Reynolds. Fox was a nephew of Lady Louisa Conolly.*

Henry Fox, 1st Lord Holland (1705-74). Portrait by Allan Ramsay. He was Lady Louisa's brother-in-law and father of Charles James Fox.*

Henry Fox, 1st Lord Holland. Half-length portrait by Sir Joshua Reynolds (1723-92).

Portrait of a Lady in a Blue Dress, possibly Katherine Conolly, by Charles Jervas (1675-1739).*

Speaker John Ponsonby, by Jacob Ennis (1728-70). Ponsonby was one of Conolly's successors as Speaker of the Irish House of Commons.

View of Rathfarnham Castle, Co. Dublin, by Thomas Walmsley (1763-1806). Rathfarnham Castle was also owned by the Conolly family.

The Liffey and ruins at Castletown by Edmund Garvey (d.1806).*

FURNITURE

Pair of George III gilt pier glasses, possibly by Jackson of Dublin.*

Early Georgian Japanned cabinet, said to have been painted by Katherine Conolly as a wedding present for her niece, Molly Burton.*

Lady Louisa's mahogany writing bureau. Dating from the mid-18th century, this is one of the most important pieces of Irish furniture in the house.*

Suite of Irish George III mahogany seat furniture in the Chinese Chippendale style. Lady Louisa paid one and a half guineas for each armchair in the 1760s.*

Pair of Irish mid-Georgian brass-bound mahogany peat buckets.

The Green Drawing Room

The Green Drawing Room was the main reception room or saloon on the ground floor. Visitors could enter from both the Entrance Hall and the garden front. Like the other state rooms, it was extensively remodelled between 1764 and 1768. Originally, it was panelled in oak, much of which survives under the present silk. The influence of the published designs of Serlio and the leading British architect Isaac Ware can be seen in the neo-classical ceilings, door cases and chimney pieces. The Greek key pattern in the plasterwork is repeated in the frames of the pier glasses, the pier tables, and the chimney piece. The walls were first lined with a pale green silk damask in the 1760s. Fragments of this silk, which was replaced by a dark green mid-19th-century silk, survived and the present silk was woven as a direct colour match in 1985 by Prelle et Cie in Lyon, France.

PAINTINGS

William Conolly, by Charles Jervas (1675-1739), showing Speaker Conolly with mace of office.*
Katherine Conolly, also by Jervas, pictured with her niece, Molly Burton.*
General de Ginkel, 1st Earl of Athlone, by Jervas. Ginkel was a hero of the Williamite wars, 1689-91.*
Thomas Wentworth, 1st Earl of Strafford and his secretary, after Van Dyck. The portrait came to Castletown in 1752 with Lady Anne Conolly *nee* Wentworth. Strafford had been Lord Lieutenant of Ireland under Charles I.*

FURNITURE

An Irish George II bookcase, with glazed front, made c.1740 for Castletown.*
Pair of original George III giltwood mirrors by Jackson of Dublin.*
Pair of Regency style giltwood tables with Greek key pattern. Modern copies of Castletown originals.*
Fine suite of Irish early Georgian mahogany seat furniture upholstered in French floral tapestry, originally from Headfort, Co. Meath.
A George III decorative musical clock, made by Charles Clay of London. This formerly stood in the hall at Castletown.*

OPPOSITE: Details from the Print Room walls including Lady Sarah Lennox sacrificing to the Graces after Reynolds; David Garrick between the Muses of tragedy and comedy; and Van Dyck's portrait of the children of Charles I.

The Print Room

The Print Room is one of the most important rooms at Castletown. It is the only fully intact 18th-century print room left in Ireland. During Lady Louisa's time, it became popular for ladies to collect their favourite prints and arrange and paste them onto the walls of a chosen room, along with decorative borders. In 1768, Lady Louisa, together with her sister Sarah, decorated this former anteroom with prints she had been collecting since at least 1762. The Print Room can be seen as a scrapbook of mid-18th-century culture and taste. Included among the prints is Sir Joshua Reynolds' portrait of Lady Louisa's sister Sarah, sacrificing herself to the Graces. Continuing the family theme, the north wall features a print after Van Dyck of the children of Charles I, including the future Charles II, Lady Louisa's great-grandfather. Contemporary popular culture is represented by two prints of the leading actor David Garrick who is pictured between the Muses of tragedy and comedy above the fireplace. The actress Sarah Cibber is on the opposite wall.

Among the artists featured are Rembrandt, Guido Reni, Teniers and Le Bas.

Unusually, this print room survived changes in taste and fashion, although the room seems to have been slightly rearranged in the mid-19th century. In the late 19th century this room was used as a billiards room.

OPPOSITE: Group, including the 1st Duke of Leinster, skating on the River Liffey c. 1768, by Robert Healy.

The State Bedroom and The Healy Room

When the house was first laid out in the 1720s, this room, along with the rooms on either side, formed William Conolly's bedroom suite. It was intended that he would receive guests in the morning while sitting up in bed or being dressed, in the manner of the French court at Versailles. This practice did not continue after the Speaker's death in 1729, although the bed remained until at least 1825. Later, in the 19th century, it was converted into a library and the mock leather Victorian wallpaper dates from this time. Sadly, the Castletown library was dispersed in the 1960s and today the furniture reflects the room's original use.

PAINTINGS
The portraits on display feature members of the St George family from Tyrone House, Co. Galway. Included are three portraits of the St George children by John Ryan of Galway.

FURNITURE
Set of four late 18th-century Venetian chairs.
Flemish 17th-century rosewood table-cabinet on an Irish 18th-century stand.
Early 18th-century Italian silk tester bedstead.
Mid-19th-century Louis Phillipe Aubusson carpet.*

The Healy Room

This room originally served as a dressing room or closet attached to the State Bedroom. It was used as a small sitting room and later became Major Edward Conolly's bedroom in the mid-20th century as it was one of the few rooms that could be kept warm in winter. It is now known as the Healy Room after the pictures of the Castletown horses by the Irish artist Robert Healy (d.1771). Today, photographic reproductions hang in the place of the original drawings. The original grisaille drawings date from c.1768 and feature the Castletown racehorses, huntsmen and portraits of both Thomas Conolly and Lady Louisa with their horses and surveying their demesne.

The Map Room

The Map Room is another of the 18 closets in the house. Today, this panelled room houses a small collection of maps, including two demesne maps dating from 1739 and 1768 respectively, which show some of the changes made to the Castletown demesne by Lady Louisa in the mid-18th century. Also hanging is a copy of Noble and Keenan's map of Co. Kildare (1752), which features vignettes of the Conolly Folly, Carton and Leixlip Castle.

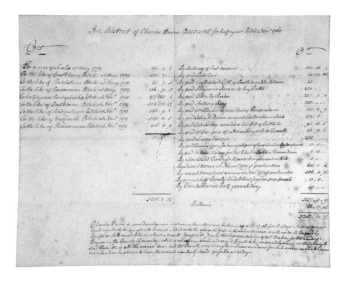

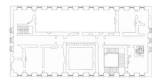

The Long Gallery

The Long Gallery is one of the most celebrated rooms at Castletown, and indeed, in Ireland. Originally intended as a picture gallery linked to flanking rooms on the north front, it was described by John Loveday, an English visitor in 1732, as follows: *'Here is a length of the Duke of Wharton, another of the Duke of Grafton, lord lieutenant and his Duchess, but a remarkably good length painting of Lord Chancellor West in his robes. There are a large number of prints here and some antique seals taken off in wax and put into glass picture cases. No tapestry but what was made in Dublin, the figures are small, the colours are very lively.'*

This preference for a formal long gallery was very much in vogue in the 1720s, but had become old-fashioned by the time Lady Louisa arrived at Castletown. Initially, in 1760, she rearranged the layout by removing the original doorways to the upper east and west corridors, replacing them with the central doorway above the Entrance Hall. The new doorcases as well as new fireplaces at either end were designed by leading English architect, Sir William Chambers, while the work was again overseen by Simon Vierpyl. The Pompeian style decoration dates from the 1770s, and was inspired by Montfaucon's publications on the

excavations at Pompeii and Herculaneum and Raphael's designs for the Vatican. Among the themes illustrated are love, marriage and family as well as subjects from antiquity. The decoration is by an English artist and engraver, Charles Ruben Riley, (1752-98), assisted by Englishman, Thomas Ryder, (1746-1810). The ceiling was also painted in Lady Louisa's time to match the walls. The lunette, depicting Aurora, Goddess of the Dawn, above the doorway is after a painting by Guido Reni in Rome. The three Murano chandeliers were specially imported from Venice in the 1770s.

The Long Gallery became a space for informal entertaining unlike the grand state rooms downstairs. It was full of furniture, much of which remained in the 1890s, including four Chippendale sofas, a gilded Louis XIV high-backed sofa and Lady Louisa's Broadwood piano dating from 1796. It was also full of life and activity as the following

PAINTINGS

Lady Louisa Conolly (1743-1821), after Sir Joshua Reynolds (1723-92).* Original in Fogg Art Museum, Harvard.

Thomas Conolly (1738-1803). Photographic copy of portrait by Anton Raphael Mengs (1728-78), painted while Conolly was in Rome on his Grand Tour.* Original in National Gallery of Ireland.

FURNITURE

Set of four Louis XVI French giltwood mirrors.*
George III library armchairs, part of a set purchased by Lady Louisa for Castletown in the 1760s.*
Important set of eight giltwood consoles probably designed by Sir William Chambers for Castletown.*

SCULPTURE

Set of eight marble busts of classical figures attributed to Simon Vierpyl, late 18th century.*
17th-century marble statue of Diana, goddess of the hunt, in centre niche, possibly purchased by Thomas Conolly on his Grand Tour.*
Two early 19th-century busts of classical warriors on blue and white marble pedestals.*
Two early 19th-century busts of Apollo Belvedere and Pallas Athene on red and white marble pedestals.*

excerpt from one of Lady Louisa's letters suggests: *'Our gallery was in great vogue, and really is a charming room for there is such a variety of occupations in it, that people cannot be formal in it…Lord Harcourt was writing, some of us played at whist, others at billiards, Mrs Gardiner at the harpsichord, others at chess, others at reading and supper at one end. I have seldom seen twenty people in a room so easily disposed of….'* It was also frequently used for theatrical performances, often involving members of the family and their acquaintances. In recent times, this tradition has been continued, with the room a regular venue for concerts and other performances.

The room has seen few changes since Lady Louisa's time. The ceiling and the blue background on the walls were repainted in the 19th century (it was originally grey), while major conservation work was carried out on the decorative paintwork in 1989.

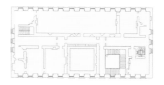

The Pastel Room

The Pastel Room or the Grey Room was originally an anteroom to the adjoining Long Gallery. It was used as a schoolroom in the 19th century when children became a feature of Castletown life for the first time. It is known as the Pastel Room today because of the fine collection of pastel portraits. These portraits include a splendid pastel of Lady Louisa's father, Charles Lennox, 2nd Duke of Richmond, painted by the fashionable Venetian artist, Rosalba Carriera, while he was on his Grand Tour. The smaller pastels surrounding the fireplace include some by the leading 18th-century Irish pastel artist, Hugh Douglas Hamilton. These include a pair of portraits of Thomas and Lady Louisa Conolly. Among the other figures pictured are Charles James Fox and the Staples sisters, including Louisa Staples, whose son Edward Pakenham inherited Castletown upon Lady Louisa's death in 1821.

PAINTINGS
Earl of March, later 2nd Duke of Richmond. Pastel portrait of Lady Louisa's father by Rosalba Carriera (1675-1757).*
Countess of March, later Duchess of Richmond, pastel portrait of Lady Louisa's mother attributed to the circle of George Knapton (1698-1778).*
Lady Louisa aged four, attributed to circle of George Knapton.*
Thomas and Lady Louisa Conolly, Charles James Fox, Hussey Burgh, Staples sisters; oval pastel portraits by Hugh Douglas Hamilton (1739-1808).*

FURNITURE
George II Irish walnut side table with moulded Kilkenny limestone top' .*

47

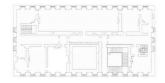

The Boudoir

The Boudoir and the adjoining two rooms formed Lady Louisa's personal apartment. The Boudoir served as a private sitting room for Lady Louisa and subsequent ladies of the house. The painted ceiling, dado rail and window shutters probably date from the late 18th century, and were restored in the 1970s by artist Philippa Garner. The wall panels or grotesques, after Raphael, date from the mid-19th century and formerly hung in the Long Gallery. Among the items inside the modern, built-in glass cabinet are pieces of glass and china featuring the Conolly crest.

PAINTINGS
Ten Grotesques. Mid-19th century after Raphael and school.*

FURNITURE
Built-in glass fronted cabinet. Items inside include silver and glassware engraved with the Conolly crest, examples of 18th-century Irish bookbindings, including copies of the Commons Journals, and a set of bookbinding tools. *
Irish mahogany green baize lined card table. *
Giltwood mirror of Chinese Chippendale style.
Suite of Louis XVI chairs, upholstered in Beauvais tapestry, formerly of Luttrellstown Castle.
Two George III style commodes.

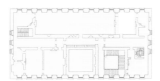

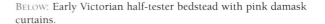
BELOW: Early Victorian half-tester bedstead with pink damask curtains.

The Blue Bedroom

The Blue Bedroom provides a fine example of an early Victorian bedroom. Like the Boudoir, it forms part of an apartment with two adjoining dressing rooms. The principal bedrooms, used by family and honoured guests, were on this floor. Bedrooms on the upper floor were also used for guests and for children, while the servants slept in the basement.

PAINTINGS

Lady Harriet St George (1782-1830). Three-quarter length portrait of the Irish school.
La Moue. Pastel after Goya by Harriet Hockley-Townshend (1877-1941).
Summer. Pastel by Harriet Hockley-Townshend.
Portrait of girl in a white dress by Harriet Hockley-Townshend.
Winter, 1911. Portrait of Miss Theodisia Townsend by Harriet Hockley-Townshend.

FURNITURE

Early Victorian half-tester bedstead with pink damask curtains.
Pair of early Victorian giltwood drawing room chairs carved with Conolly crest and monogram of Tom Conolly c. 1850.*

BELOW TOP: Vignette of the Obelisk taken from the 1752 Noble and Keenan map of Kildare.
BELOW BOTTOM: Detail from the Noble and Keenan map of 1752 showing the location of the Obelisk in relation to Castletown House.

The Conolly Folly or Obelisk

My Sister is now building an obleix to answer a vistow from the bake of Castletown house; it will cost her three or four hundred pounds at least, but I believe more. I really wonder how she can dow so much and live as she duse.

Mary Jones March 1740

Visible from the windows in the Long Gallery, the Conolly Folly or Obelisk closes the two-mile vista at the rear of the house. It may have been designed by the German architect Richard Castle (1695-1751), who was working at nearby Carton for the Earl of Kildare. This singular piece of Irish architecture stands 140 feet tall with a soaring obelisk supported by a series of arches beneath. Standing on part of the Carton estate, it was built in 1740 by Katherine Conolly to provide employment for the starving Castletown tenantry during the severe winter and subsequent famine of 1739/40. Intended to mark the boundary of the Castletown demesne, it actually stood on part of the Carton estate. Dominating the local landscape, it became a focal point for both the Castletown and Carton demesnes. Thanks to the generosity of Mrs Rose Saul-Zalles, it was acquired in a ruinous state in 1960 by the recently reconstituted Irish Georgian Society, and its restoration was their first major project. In 1989, Mariga Guinness, one of the Society's co-founders, was buried beneath one of the side arches. It is now in the care of the Office of Public Works.

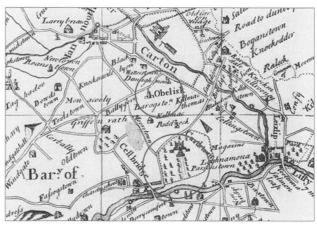

The Wonderful Barn

This unusual corkscrew shaped building was built in 1743 to close the vista to the east of Castletown. The only similar building in Ireland is the bottle-tower near Rathfarnham in Co. Dublin, also, incidentally, a Conolly estate. Built at a time of famine, it was used to store grain. A stone staircase winds around the outside leading to the top. Inside, each floor has a hole in the centre allowing the grain to pass through. Two smaller structures of a similar design, used as dovecotes, stand behind the main barn structure. While the Barn closed the eastern vista, the vista to the west was closed by the Celbridge Charter school (c.1730), built from funds left in Speaker Conolly's will. It is now the Setanta House Hotel.

The Conolly Monument and the Death House

The Conolly Monument was erected in 1736 by Katherine Conolly in memory of her husband, William Conolly. It stood in a mausoleum attached to the old ruined Protestant church in Celbridge village. It features splendidly carved life-sized marble figures of both the Speaker and his widow carved by the London-based sculptor, Thomas Carter the Elder (d.1757), now removed for safekeeping to Castletown. The architectural setting has been attributed to the leading Irish-based funerary sculptor, William Kidwell (1662-1736). It features a marble plaque describing William Conolly's virtues and achievements including the assertion that he had made 'a modest though splendid use of his great riches.' In total, the monument and the erection of the Death House or mausoleum to accommodate it (the existing church was too small) cost his widow the not so modest sum of £2,000.

The Castletown Demesne

At Castletown Lady Louisa ….has by the strength of her own native elegance of taste and genius for rural design improved a spot by nature infertile of beauty or elegance into a seat that when completed will be one of the most delightful rural situations outside Dublin.'
John Bush *Hibernia Curiosa* (1769)

Lady Louisa's influence at Castletown can be seen not only inside the house but also in the carefully laid-out parkland that surrounds the house. Castletown in the 18th century did not have formal flower gardens. Instead, formally laid-out landscapes in the French Baroque style were popular during this period. Alterations to the landscape at Castletown began during Katherine Conolly's stewardship of the estate, under the influence of Lady Anne Conolly, who was influenced by her father's work at Wentworth Castle in Yorkshire. Vistas connecting the house to the Wonderful Barn and the Folly were created, while early demesne maps also show a pond at the rear of the house and clearly marked meandering pathways through the woodland behind. But it was only with the arrival of Lady Louisa in 1759 that the Castletown landscape began to be radically altered in line with contemporary fashion. Influenced by the improvements made by her sister Emily, Duchess of Leinster at Carton, Lady Louisa turned to the Castletown parkland. The river Liffey to the south of the house became the focal point of the demesne. A walk was

created along the banks of the river, while rapids were created in the river to add to the picturesque quality. A number of garden buildings were also constructed. These included a Classical style temple complete with columns removed from the Long Gallery during its redecoration in the 1760s. This temple, visible from the south front of the house, was erected in honour of the actress, Sarah Siddons. Further along the river, a bathing house, now in ruins, was built to designs drawn up by Lady Louisa herself, although how much bathing actually took place is unknown.

The 18th-century Castletown landscape has survived remarkably well. It is still possible to wander along Lady Louisa's river walks and see her temple and the remains of the bathing house. In the 19th century, efforts were concentrated on the immediate environs of the house, with the creation of a formal garden behind the house and the planting of the yew trees to the front. The break-up of the estate in the 1960s, however, meant that the immense walled gardens, formerly situated to the north-west of the house, were built upon. By the early 20th century, these kitchen gardens were the most profitable aspect of the estate and a great source of local employment. The farmyard beyond the west wing remains. Formerly detached from the estate it is now in state care and undergoing restoration.

The Batty Langley Lodge

Gate lodges marked the end of each avenue at Castletown. The most interesting of these lodges is the Batty Langley Lodge which stood at the entrance to the estate from the Dublin road. The present lodge, which was influenced by the published designs of English architect and gardener, Batty Langley (1696-1751), was completed in 1785. The gothic facade reflected the contemporary vogue for the gothic in garden design. The lodge was unusual in its design as the stylised gothic facade faced towards the estate and Castletown rather than towards the road. This reflected its dual purpose. It would serve the practical function of a gate lodge, as well as serving as the end point of the river walk along the Liffey. It has also been suggested that Lady Louisa Conolly used the lodge as a cottage ornée, where she could pretend to lead a life of domestic simplicity. Other garden cottages such as the Shell House at her sister Emily's house at Carton, were used in this fashion. The planting of a shrubbery and fruit trees around the lodge reflected Lady Louisa's ideal of rustic simplicity. The primary function of the lodge, however, was to act as a gatehouse, and as a residence for one Castletown's groundsmen or gardeners, which

it did until the mid-20th century. The lodge and the surrounding grounds were detached from the remainder of the demesne in 1967, but have been recently been purchased by the Office of Public Works and have been reintegrated into the demesne.

List of benefactors of furnishings and paintings to Castletown

Includes those who have loaned items to the house as well as those who have gifted furniture and paintings to the Castletown Foundation.

Mrs Douglas Auchincloss of New York
Mrs Edith Baker of New York
Mrs George F. Baker of New York
Mr John Bereman of Chicago
The Brady Foundation
The Patrick and Aimee Butler Foundation of St Paul Minnesota
Miss Honor Crosbie Ballyheigue Castle, Co. Kerry
Dallas and Cleveland Chapters of the IGS
Sir Paul Getty
Irish Georgian Society (IGS)
Samuel H. Kress Foundation
Mr T.K. Laidlaw
London Chapter of the IGS
Mrs Annabelle Montague-Smith
Mrs Dean Perry of Chicago
Mr and Mrs Walter Pharr of New York
Gordon St George Mark of Chicago
Lord Rossmore
Mrs Tausch, Co. Cork
Mr and Mrs Galen Weston
Lady Edith Windham of Dartrey
Mrs Rose Saul Zalles of Washington

Further Reading

Barnard, Toby. 'A tale of three sisters: Katherine Conolly of Castletown' in Barnard, Toby (ed.) *Irish protestants, ascents and descents* (Dublin, 2004).

Boylan, Lena. 'The Conollys of Castletown' in *Quarterly Bulletin of the Irish Georgian Society*, vol. XI, no. 4 (1968).

Craig, Maurice and Fitzgerald, Desmond. 'Castletown, Co. Kildare' in *Country Life*, vol. CXLV (1969).

Griffin, David. 'Castletown, Co. Kildare: the contribution of James, 1st Duke of Leinster' in *Irish architectural and decorative studies*, vol. 1 (1998) pp. 120-146.

Kelleher, Ann Margaret. 'The long gallery of Castletown house' in *Quarterly Bulletin of the Irish Georgian Society*, vol. XXII (1979).

Moore, Christopher. 'Lady Louisa Conolly, mistress of Castletown, 1759-1821' in Fenlon, Jane, Figgis, Nicola and Marshall, Catherine (eds) *New perspectives in art history in honour of Anne Crookshank* (Dublin, 1987).

O'Kane, Finola. *Landscape design in 18th-century Ireland, mixing foreign trees with the natives* (Cork, 2004).

Tillyard, Stella. *Aristocrats, Caroline, Emily, Louisa and Sarah Lennox, 1740-1832* (London, 1994).

Text credits

P. 3: Quotation from Twiss, Richard, *A tour in Ireland in 1775* (London, 1776) p. 65.

P. 5: George Berkeley to John Percival, 29 July 1722 in Luce, A.A. and Jessop, T.E., *The Works of George Berkeley* (Edinburgh, 1948-57) vol. VIII, p. 123.

P. 12: Lady Llanover, *The Autobiography and Correspondence of Mary Granville, Mrs Delany* (London, 1861) vol. III, p. 282.

P. 14: Quoted in Moore, Christopher, 'Lady Louisa Conolly, mistress of Castletown, 1759-1821' in Fenlon, Jane, Figgis, Nicola and Marshall, Christopher (eds) *New perspectives in art history in honour of Anne Crookshank* (Dublin 1987) p. 139.

P. 16: Quoted in Andrew, Tod and Pelley, Patricia (eds) *Elizabeth Grant of Rothiemurchus: the highland lady in Dublin, 1851-56* (Edinburgh, 2005) p. 129.

P. 18: Elizabeth, Countess of Fingall, *Seventy Years Young: Memoirs of Elizabeth, Countess of Fingall* (Dublin, 1991) p. 415.

P. 23: Quoted in Harris, John, 'C.R. Cockerell's Ichnographica Domestica' in *Architectural History*, vol. 14 (1971) p. 12.

P. 27: Lady Llanover (ed.) *The Autobiography and Correspondence of Mary Granville, Mrs Delany* (London, 1861) vol. III, p. 282.

Lady Louisa quoted in Moore, Christopher, 'Lady Louisa Conolly, mistress of Castletown, 1759-1821' in Fenlon, Jane, Figgis, Nicola and Marshall, Catherine (eds) *New perspectives in art history in honour of Anne Crookshank* (Dublin, 1987) p. 130.

P. 33: Diary of Lady Shelburne, quoted in Griffin, David, 'Castletown, Co. Kildare: the contribution of James, 1st Duke of Leinster' in *Irish architectural and decorative studies*, vol. I (1998) p. 133.

P. 43: Quotation from Loveday, John, *Diary of a tour in 1732 through part of England, Wales, Ireland and Scotland made by John Loveday of Caversham* (Edinburgh, 1890) p. 48.

P. 46: Lady Louisa to her sister Emily, Duchess of Leinster, 6 January 1786, in Fitzgerald, Brian (ed.) *Correspondence of Emily, Duchess of Leinster* (Dublin, 1957) vol. III, p. 181.

P. 51: Mary Jones to Jane Bonnell, March 1740, quoted in Boylan, Lena, 'The Conollys of Castletown' in *Quarterly Bulletin of the Irish Georgian Society*, vol. XI, no. 4 (1968) p. 14.

P. 53: Quotation from Bush, John, *Hibernia Curiosa* (London, 1769) p. 147.

Photo credits

Con Brogan, photographer, and Tony Roche and Patricia Keenan of the Photographic Unit, Department of the Environment, Heritage and Local Government:
2, 7r, 11, 20, 23, 24, 25, 26, 31, 32, 36, 38, 39, 40, 44-5, 46, 48, 49, 53.
David Davison: 6, 9, 10, 12, 13, 14, 17, 18, 21, 22, 27, 28, 29, 33, 34, 35, 37 (left), 41, 42, 43, 47, 49 (right), 50.
Courtesy of the Shuldar-Shaw Family: 7l, 16, 18, 19, 34 (left).
Gothic Architecture Improved by Rules and Projections in Many Grand Designs... by B&T Langley, London 1747, plate LVII: 54.

All efforts have been made to trace copyright holders of all images used.